Mark Gostling

HOW COMPUTERS WORK

You do not need to know how a computer works in order to use one. But computers are fascinating, both in the way they work and in the way they are manufactured. If you make the effort to understand what goes on inside computers you will find them easier to use. *You* will be in control. This book tells you what the various parts of a computer system do, how they work, and how they are made.

Ian Litterick is an expert on microcomputer systems, a writer and an inventor. Chris Smithers has long experience of illustrating computers. Both the author and designer share an interest in helping non-experts to understand, and so to control, computer technology.

The Age of Computers

HOW COMPUTERS WORK

Ian Litterick
Designed by Chris Smithers

Other books in this series

Computers in Everyday Life
The Story of Computers
Computers and You
Robots and Intelligent Machines
Programming Computers

ISBN 0 85078 257 0

© Copyright 1983 Wayland (Publishers) Limited
First published in 1983 by
Wayland (Publishers) Limited
49 Lansdowne Place, Hove,
East Sussex BN3 1HF, England

Second impression 1984

Third impression 1985

Typeset in the U.K. by Dialogue
Printed in Italy by G. Canale & C. S.p.A., Turin
Bound in the U.K. at the Pitman Press, Bath

Contents

What is a computer?

A computer is a machine which gets information, changes, organizes, and stores it, and puts out new information when it is wanted.

The word 'computer' suggests that computers are made solely for the purpose of making computations or complicated calculations. With the early computers this was certainly the case. Now, however, they deal not only with numbers, but also with other kinds of information.

Information passes through a computer in four stages. It enters a computer as input, is organized by the processor and stored, and comes out in a new form as output. The input a computer gets can be, for example, characters typed in through a keyboard, temperature readings relayed from a sensor, numbers keyed in from a pad, or computer data sent via a telephone line.

The processor, or central processing unit (CPU), then organizes this information. It does this with the help of the programs and data held in its store or memory. Programs are the instructions the processor needs to tell it what to do, while data is the information the computer has been given.

To organize the information, the computer may move it around in its memory many times, using both its temporary memory (which it can get at very quickly), and its permanent memory (where the information will stay even when the computer is turned off) to complete its task.

Then, when the computer's instructions tell it to do so, it outputs the new information on to a TV screen or a printer. It can also instruct a motor to start or a machine to operate.

A word processor usually gets information typed in through a keyboard. It changes that information and stores it

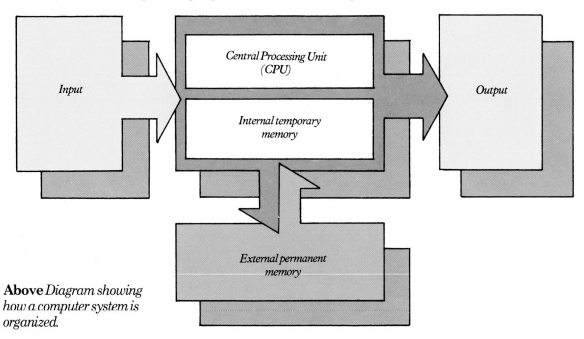

Above *Diagram showing how a computer system is organized.*

according to its program, and according to the instructions which are input at the keyboard. Typewritten pages are then printed when they are required.

A computer game gets input from its coin mechanism, buttons, and joystick. It then processes that information according to the instructions stored in the program, and it outputs the result in the form of pictures on a screen, sound effects and a score.

The computer in a washing machine gets input from the keys or buttons and from its own sensors, and processes this information according to the manufacturer's programs. It then outputs signals to control the motors which make the drum revolve, heat the water, and pump the water in and out.

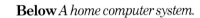
Below *A home computer system.*

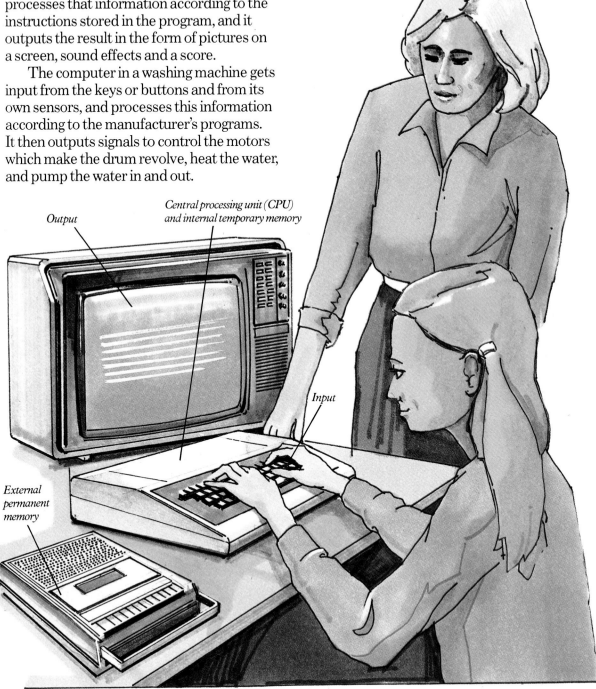

Output

Central processing unit (CPU) and internal temporary memory

Input

External permanent memory

7

The parts of a computer system

A computer may have only one means of input and one of output – a keyboard for input and a screen for output, for example. Alternatively, a computer may have a wide range of input and output devices, like the microcomputer illustrated below. Some of them may be in the same box as the computer itself. Or they may be separate, in which case they are called peripherals.

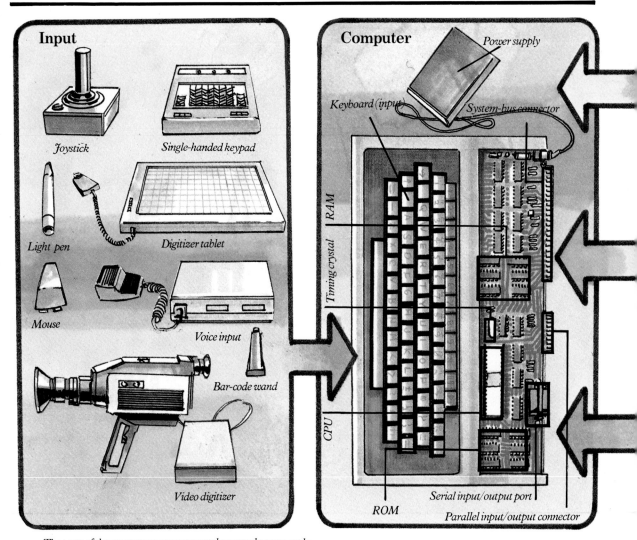

Input

Joystick

Single-handed keypad

Light pen

Digitizer tablet

Mouse

Voice input

Bar-code wand

Video digitizer

Computer

Power supply

Keyboard (input)

System-bus connector

RAM

Timing crystal

CPU

ROM

Serial input/output port

Parallel input/output connector

The parts of the computer system are not shown to the same scale.

Output

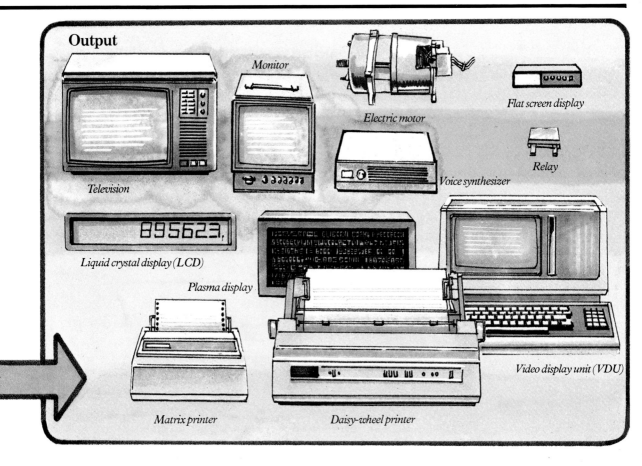

Monitor

Electric motor

Flat screen display

Relay

Television

Voice synthesizer

Liquid crystal display (LCD)

895623,

Plasma display

Video display unit (VDU)

Matrix printer

Daisy-wheel printer

External permanent memory

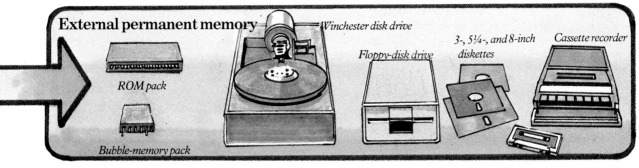

Winchester disk drive

Floppy-disk drive

3-, 5¼-, and 8-inch diskettes

Cassette recorder

ROM pack

Bubble-memory pack

Communications

Acoustic coupler

Receiver

Transmitter

Cable

Modem

Fibre optics

The processor: the heart of the system

At the heart of a microcomputer system is the processor itself, the CPU or central processing unit. It is sealed in a plastic or ceramic box about 5 cm (2 in) long and 2 cm (0.75 in) wide, and it controls the whole system.

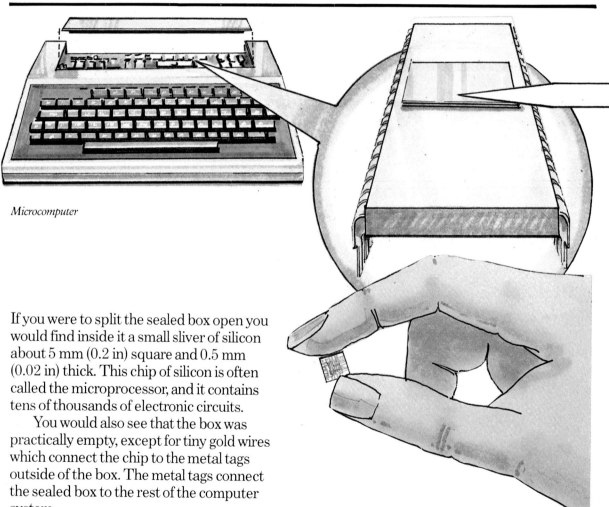

Microcomputer

If you were to split the sealed box open you would find inside it a small sliver of silicon about 5 mm (0.2 in) square and 0.5 mm (0.02 in) thick. This chip of silicon is often called the microprocessor, and it contains tens of thousands of electronic circuits.

You would also see that the box was practically empty, except for tiny gold wires which connect the chip to the metal tags outside of the box. The metal tags connect the sealed box to the rest of the computer system.

The processor has many different functions. It has to 'talk' to the rest of the system, so there is an input/output area on the chip which deals with that. There is a

Top *The complete microprocessor package.*
Above *A microprocessor chip is only 5mm (0.2 in) square.*
Opposite page *A close-up view of the microprocessor chip.*

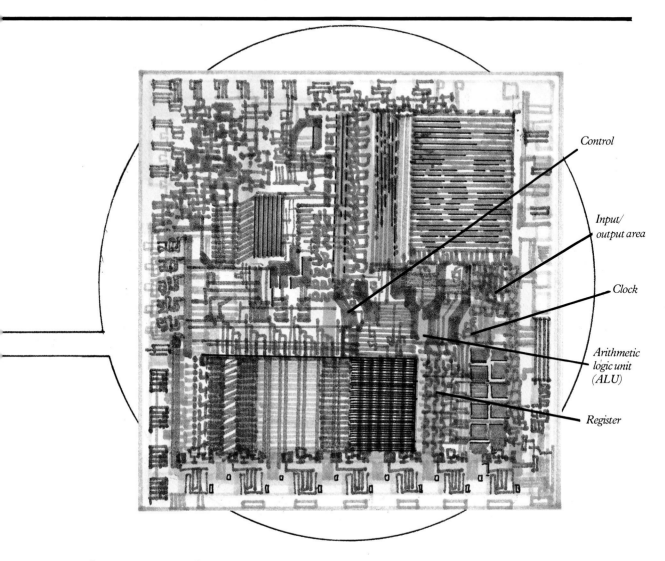

Control

Input/ output area

Clock

Arithmetic logic unit (ALU)

Register

control area to oversee the operation of the rest of the chip. There is also a clock, sometimes separate from the rest of the chip, which produces several million electronic pulses a second to beat time, so that all the parts of the system can do their work in step with each other. Then there are registers where the processor stores the information it is working on.

Perhaps the most important part of the microprocessor is the arithmetic and logic unit (ALU). It is the ALU which, doing only four simple things, changes and organizes the information flowing into and out of the microprocessor. It adds pieces of information to each other, subtracts them, moves them

into and out of storage, and compares them with each other. Although it can only do four things, it does them many thousands of times a second, so it can organize information many thousands of times faster than a human could hope to do.

There may be more than one microprocessor in a computer system. Input/output devices often have their own microprocessor chips dedicated to serving their needs, getting the information in, arranging it and then putting it out. For example, the microcomputer in a printer gets input, arranges and organizes it, and outputs signals to move the paper and to print the characters.

Bits, bytes and binary: how computers deal with information

Each electronic circuit in a computer is in one of two states. Either it is on, or it is off. And that is the only way it can process information.

Electronic circuits can switch very rapidly indeed from one state (on) to another state (off). The computer uses these two states to signify a bit of information. On can equal 1 and off can equal 0. Each bit of information is indeed called a bit, which is short for binary digit, although you might like to think of it as the smallest 'bit' of information the computer can deal with.

Rather than dealing with one bit at a time, computers and microprocessors usually deal with 8 or 16 bits at once. As you can imagine, this enables them to work much faster. Using patterns of 7 or 8 bits, each one switched off as a 0 or on as a 1, the computer can signify all the letters of the alphabet.

The American Standard Code for Information Interchange (ASCII – pronounced 'askey') is a pattern of 7 bits, because with 7 bits you can signify 128 different characters (that's 2 to the power of 7). 128 is enough different combinations to express all the characters that we commonly use. It includes all the small letters, all the capital letters, the numbers, different

Right *How a computer represents a bit of information (top), and how bits of information can be arranged in a pattern of 8 or 16 bits.*

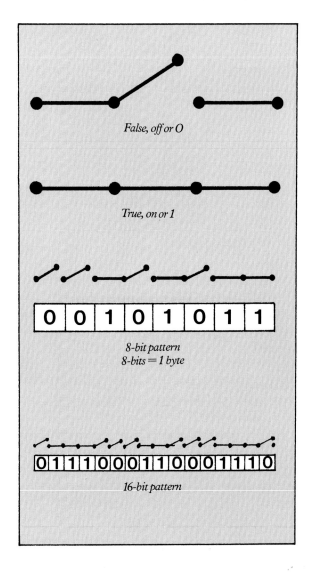

False, off or 0

True, on or 1

| 0 | 0 | 1 | 0 | 1 | 0 | 1 | 1 |

8-bit pattern
8-bits = 1 byte

| 0 | 1 | 1 | 1 | 0 | 0 | 0 | 1 | 1 | 0 | 0 | 0 | 1 | 1 | 1 | 0 |

16-bit pattern

Decimal	Binary								Hexadecimal	
0	0	0	0	0	0	0	0	0	0	0
1	0	0	0	0	0	0	0	1	0	1
2	0	0	0	0	0	0	1	0	0	2
3	0	0	0	0	0	0	1	1	0	3
4	0	0	0	0	0	1	0	0	0	4
5	0	0	0	0	0	1	0	1	0	5
6	0	0	0	0	0	1	1	0	0	6
7	0	0	0	0	0	1	1	1	0	7
8	0	0	0	0	1	0	0	0	0	8
9	0	0	0	0	1	0	0	1	0	9
10	0	0	0	0	1	0	1	0	0	A
11	0	0	0	0	1	0	1	1	0	B
12	0	0	0	0	1	1	0	0	0	C
13	0	0	0	0	1	1	0	1	0	D
14	0	0	0	0	1	1	1	0	0	E
15	0	0	0	0	1	1	1	1	0	F
16	0	0	0	1	0	0	0	0	1	0
48	0	0	1	1	0	0	0	0	3	0

punctuation marks, characters for controlling the computer, and even a character for a space.

The 8-bit chunk which the microcomputer generally deals in is called a byte.

With our 0's and 1's we can count to and signify numbers. Instead of carrying to another digit every time we reach a power of 10, as we do with the decimal system which we usually count in, we add another digit every time we get to a power of 2. This is called the binary system, or counting to base two. So, instead of writing numbers as units, tens, hundreds, etc., as we do with ordinary (decimal) numbers, binary numbers are written as units, twos, fours, eights, etc. For example, the decimal number 13 = 1 ten and 3 units; the binary number 1101 = 1 eight, 1 four, no twos and 1 unit = 13 (decimal).

Using an 8-bit byte we can count up to 255 (11111111 in binary) – 256 different numbers if you include 0. And using 16 bits – 2 bytes – we can count up to 65,535.

By using a larger number of bytes in which to store a number, even the smallest microcomputer can deal with very large numbers indeed.

Because binary numbers are difficult to remember, computer people count with base 16 (hexadecimal or HEX), using the characters 0-9 and A-F (for the numbers 10-15). 'F' is 15, so FF is 225. A byte can always be written in two characters.

Left *A table showing some decimal numbers with their binary and hexadecimal equivalent. The binary and hexadecimal numbers are 1 byte long.*

Decision-making by transistor

We have seen how numbers and letters can be represented by 0's and 1's, but how does a computer use the same system of 0's and 1's to make decisions?

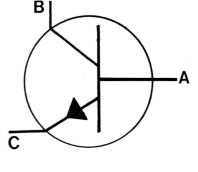

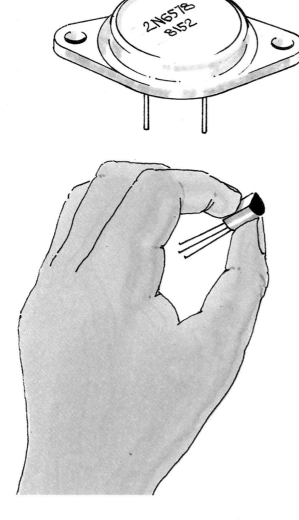

Above *Two types of transistor and their electrical symbol.*

The processor uses the 0's and 1's – the presence or absence of electric current – to operate switches. These switches are called transistors, and they have no mechanically moving parts.

A transistor is made out of a semi-conductor. A conductor is something which conducts electricity —steel, carbon or copper, for example. An insulator, on the other hand, is something which does not conduct electricity —paper, rubber, most plastics, or glass, for example. You can get an electric shock from live metal (a conductor which has electricity running through it), and you can protect yourself from electric shock by putting rubber (an insulator) between yourself and the electricity.

A semi-conductor is something between the two. This means that it can be controlled, usually by electricity, so that sometimes it conducts electricity and sometimes it does not.

By putting transistors together in different orders, a number of different controls, or logic gates, can be created. Two common controls are the 'AND' and 'OR' gates. An AND gate switches electricity through only if both its wires coming in are switched on. An OR gate switches electricity through if either one wire or the other or both wires are switched on. This system is called Boolean logic, after George Boole, who invented it. It enables computers to carry out complex instructions despite only being able to deal with two states – on and off.

When a number of transistors are combined into one package, this is called an integrated circuit or chip. Very large scale integration (VLSI) circuits have as many as a million components on them, which include not only transistors, but also resistors and capacitors.

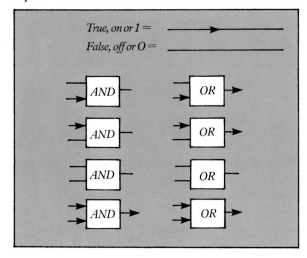

Above *Diagram showing how AND and OR gates control the flow of electricity.*

Right *Using security systems as an example, these diagrams show how logic circuits can be constructed using AND and OR gates:*

1 *If the door is open* and *the alarm is switched on the bell will ring.*

2 *If the door is open* and *the alarm is switched off the bell will not ring.*

3,4 *If either the door* or *the window or both are open* and *the alarm is switched on the bell will ring.*

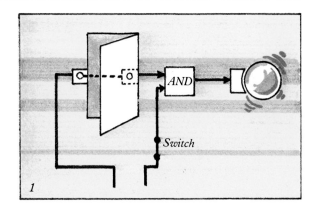

1

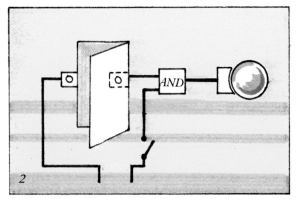

2

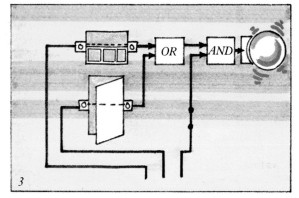

3

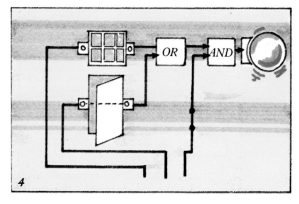

4

Making silicon chips

Silicon chips need to be made with the greatest care and accuracy. The process of making chips is very well organized and tightly controlled. This helps to keep the price of some of the simpler chips down to no more than a couple of packets of chewing gum.

The main material used to make silicon chips is, of course, silicon, and silicon is made from a pure type of sand. The sand is melted at 1,420°C (2,588°F), and a seed of pure silicon is put into the liquid and withdrawn very slowly while being turned. A crystal grows on the silicon seed to produce a long cylinder of silicon 10 cm (4 in) in diameter and 1 m (3 ft) in length. This is then sliced by a diamond saw into thin wafers, each one 0.5 mm (0.02 in) thick. One side of each wafer is then highly polished.

The wafers are then oxidized several hundred at a time in a furnace, in an atmosphere of steam. This treatment builds up a layer of silicon oxide on the surface of each wafer.

Selected areas of the silicon oxide are then etched by a photographic process, and the exposed silicon is treated with chemicals to affect the way it conducts electricity. Finally, a layer of metal is deposited on the surface and etched to produce thousands of minute circuits.

Each silicon wafer will now have etched on it many hundreds of identical chips each measuring only 5 mm (0.2 in) square. The whole process must be carried out in clean, dust-free rooms.

The silicon chips are tested by very fine probes to see that they work properly, and then they are broken from the silicon wafers to make the individual chips. Finally, each chip is sealed in its own plastic or ceramic box. Because the chips are very small and light, they can be sent to the Far East, where labour costs are relatively low, to be sealed in their boxes and then flown back to a factory for assembly into a computer.

Left *Cylinders of silicon ready for slicing into wafers.*
Opposite *How silicon chips are made.*

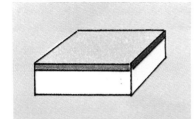

1. *The wafers of silicon are heated in an atmosphere of steam, which leaves a thin layer of oxide covering their surfaces.*

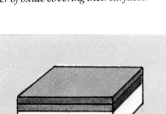

2. *The wafer is covered with a layer of photoresist (a chemical which can be softened by ultraviolet light). It is then heated to harden the photoresist.*

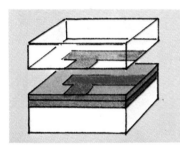

3. *Ultraviolet light is shone through a photographic 'mask' which has the pattern of perhaps 200 individual chips on it.*

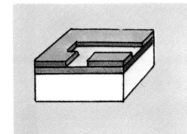

4. *The soft parts of the resist (in areas which were not masked) are removed by a solvent, and the remaining resist is heated to harden it further.*

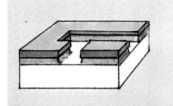

5. *The exposed areas of oxide are dissolved in hydrofluoric acid, which does not affect the photoresist or the silicon itself. Another solvent removes the resist.*

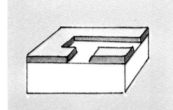

6. *In a furnace, the wafer is exposed to chemicals which penetrate the silicon through the oxide gaps to make transistors. The process is repeated several times for different layers.*

7. *A final layer of metal connects the components together, and then each chip is inspected and tested with probes. Defective ones are marked with a dot.*

8. *Lines are scored with a saw between the individual chips, which are then separated from each other. Defective ones are put to one side.*

9. *Fine wires are bonded from the circuits on the chip to the legs of the chip package, and the package is then sealed up, ready for use.*

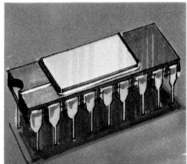

Chips that remember

A computer needs a memory that it can use quickly. The same techniques described in the last chapter are used to make RAM and ROM memory chips, which the computer uses to store programs and data.

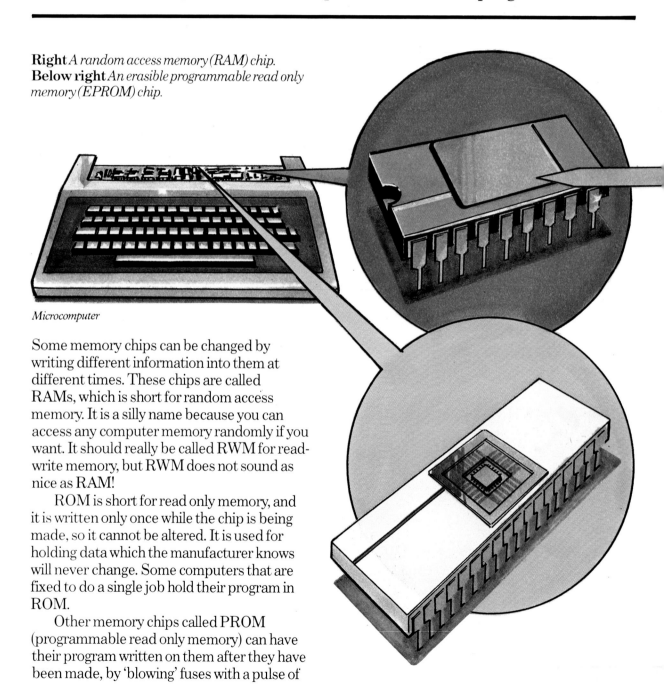

Right *A random access memory (RAM) chip.*
Below right *An erasible programmable read only memory (EPROM) chip.*

Microcomputer

Some memory chips can be changed by writing different information into them at different times. These chips are called RAMs, which is short for random access memory. It is a silly name because you can access any computer memory randomly if you want. It should really be called RWM for read-write memory, but RWM does not sound as nice as RAM!

ROM is short for read only memory, and it is written only once while the chip is being made, so it cannot be altered. It is used for holding data which the manufacturer knows will never change. Some computers that are fixed to do a single job hold their program in ROM.

Other memory chips called PROM (programmable read only memory) can have their program written on them after they have been made, by 'blowing' fuses with a pulse of

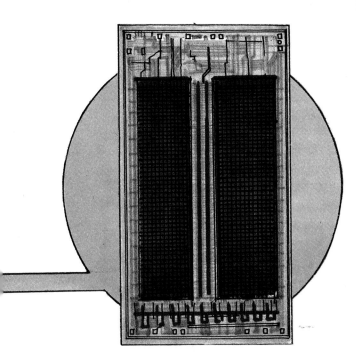

Above *Close-up of a RAM chip.*

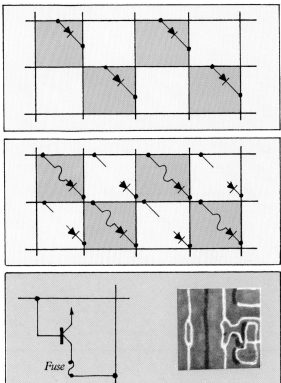

Top *Diagram of programmed memory elements in a ROM.*
Middle *The same program in a PROM.*
Bottom *The electrical symbol of a typical PROM memory element (left), and a close-up of the circuit.*

electricity. Usually these are EPROMS (erasable PROMS). With EPROMS the memory patterns can be erased by shining ultraviolet light through a little window in the package. This connects the fuses up again so that the chip can be programmed again and again.

Because EPROMS are the only chip package where you can actually see the chip itself through the window, newspapers often use EPROMS as illustrations of microprocessors. However, as you know, EPROMS are not microprocessors, but only memory chips.

EAROMS (electrically alterable ROMS) can be reprogrammed by electricity, without the bother of ultraviolet light. But each chip can only be altered a few thousand times before its ability to be reprogrammed wears out. So it cannot be used instead of a RAM chip where a bit of data may change many thousands of times a minute.

A few years ago, RAM chips could only hold a thousand bits of data (1k). Now the same size chips can hold as much as 256k, and 1 million bit chips (1 megabit) are being designed. It takes only eight 64k (bit) chips to provide the memory for a 64k (byte) computer. Remember that there are 8 bits in a byte.

Bubble memories store data on tiny moving bubbles in garnet crystal, which are read and written on as they move past. This is more expensive and slower than RAM, but it keeps its data when the power is turned off.

Single chip microcomputers have both RAM and ROM on the same chip as a processor. So one chip can contain enough electronics to enable a small computer to do its task.

Power packs, clocks, boards and cases

The chips in a microcomputer cannot work on their own. They need to be connected together; they need electricity; they need a clock to beat the time; and they need to be enclosed in a case.

Below *A power supply module.*
Bottom *The quartz timing crystal.*

Microcomputer

Microcomputers work on a small voltage of electricity. Often this is only 5 or 12 volts, compared with the 110 or 240 volts which come from the ordinary wall socket. If you plugged a chip straight into an electric socket, the chip would blow up!

So computers need a power supply. Sometimes this is just a battery or battery pack, particularly if the computer is very

small. Otherwise it is a transformer, which changes the mains voltage down to the 5 or 12 volts needed. It also converts the mains supply from alternating current to direct current, which the computer needs to switch its gates.

We have already learnt that a computer system needs a clock to beat the time, so that all the CPU and memory chips know at which

20

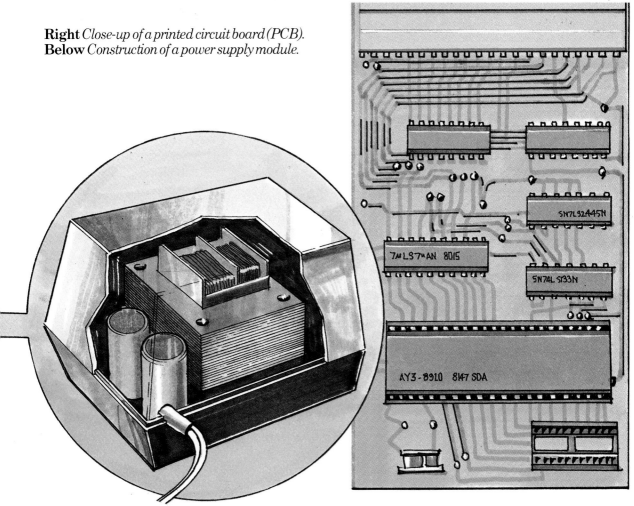

Right *Close-up of a printed circuit board (PCB).*
Below *Construction of a power supply module.*

instant to look for data and instructions. This clock is usually provided by a quartz crystal which vibrates very regularly – several millions of times a second – when an electric current is passed through it.

The chips, power supply and clock all need to be connected together. In early versions of the computer, this was done with many lengths of wire. Now, however, printed circuit boards (PCBs) are used instead.

On a PCB the 'wires' or conductors are printed on to a board made from an insulating material. To be more exact, the pattern of connections is printed on to a copper-plated board, and then the board is dipped into acid, which removes the copper except on the printed area. The copper thus

forms tracks, which conduct electricity wherever it is needed. Holes are drilled in the PCB, and the chips and other components are soldered into them.

Surprisingly, the case which encloses all the components is often the most expensive part of a computer to produce. It is made from metal or plastic and it is designed to protect the electronics, and to prevent people getting electric shocks from the live components. It is also designed to allow enough air to get in to keep the chips cool, aided perhaps by a fan, and it prevents radio waves coming from the computer, which would interfere with the reception of such electronic equipment as televisions and radios.

Permanent memory

Computer systems often need to remember much larger amounts of data and programs than they can store in RAM. They also need to remember things when their power is turned off. So they need some kind of permanent memory, separate from the computer itself.

Fortunately it is quite easy to store computer data for long periods of time. The commonest and cheapest method is to use a tape recorder and music cassette, which is connected to the computer when it is needed. But a cassette recorder is slow – it may take several minutes to read a whole program in or to find a particular piece of data.

Floppy disk drives solve the speed problem. A floppy disk drive records data on to a rapidly moving magnetic disk instead of on to a strip of cassette tape. The disks or

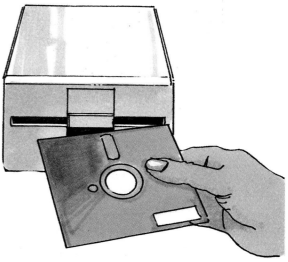

Data byte   *Control bits*

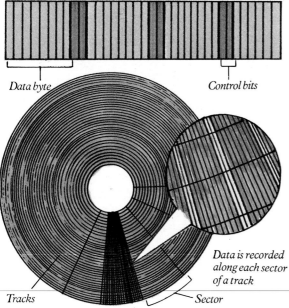

Tracks   *Sector*

Data is recorded along each sector of a track

Top left *A cassette tape memory.*
Middle left *How data is arranged on a cassette tape.*
Left *How data is arranged on a floppy disk.*
Above *A floppy disk drive. Floppy disks are always contained in a protective envelope.*
Opposite *The numbers of copies of* How Computers Work *that can be stored in different types of permanent memory.*

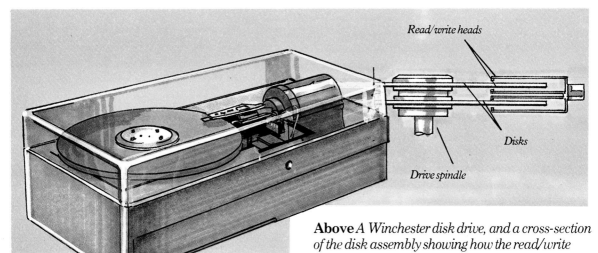

Read/write heads

Disks

Drive spindle

Above *A Winchester disk drive, and a cross-section of the disk assembly showing how the read/write heads move over both surfaces of the disk.*

'diskettes' are like records, except that they are less rigid, which is why they are called floppy disks. The data is recorded magnetically in a number of concentric tracks. To help the computer immediately find the information it wants, each track is divided up into blocks or sectors, and an index or directory of all the files on the disk is kept on the disk.

Floppy disks can contain anything from 100k bytes (or 100,000 characters – twice as much as the text in this book) to 3 megabytes (3 million bytes), depending on the size of the disk and how closely the data is packed.

There are 3-inch (75 mm), 5¼-inch (130 mm) and 8-inch (200 mm) disks. Disks can be taken from the computer and stored separately, and any amount of data can be used at different times on the same computer.

A Winchester disk drive works similarly to a floppy disk drive, except that the disk itself is rigid and mounted in a sealed box where no dirt can get in. The disk revolves very fast and the read/write head is designed aerodynamically, so that it flies a tiny distance above the surface of the disk. A 5¼-inch Winchester disk drive can hold from 5 to 25 or more megabytes of data.

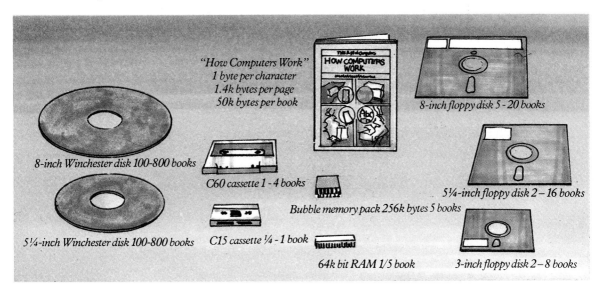

8-inch Winchester disk 100-800 books

5¼-inch Winchester disk 100-800 books

"How Computers Work"
1 byte per character
1.4k bytes per page
50k bytes per book

C60 cassette 1 - 4 books

C15 cassette ¼ - 1 book

64k bit RAM 1/5 book

Bubble memory pack 256k bytes 5 books

8-inch floppy disk 5 - 20 books

5¼-inch floppy disk 2 – 16 books

3-inch floppy disk 2 – 8 books

Keyboards

The commonest way of putting information into a microcomputer is through a keyboard. These vary from a traditional typewriter keyboard on a personal computer, to a couple of buttons on a Space Invaders game.

How does a computer know that pressing a particular keyboard key signals a particular character? Inside many keyboards there is a dedicated microprocessor connected to a matrix – a set of rows and columns – of conductors on a printed circuit board. When a key is pressed the gap between a row and a column is closed so that a pulse of electricity can pass across. This pulse is monitored by the keyboard's dedicated microprocessor, which converts the signal into the ASCII code for the character which was pressed, and sends it on to the computer.

The commonest layout for a computer keyboard is the typewriter layout, whose top row of letters runs QWERTYUIOP. Ergonomists – people who design machines so that people can use them easily – have tried to design better keyboards. One

Above *A typical microcomputer keyboard.*
Below *The Maltron ergonomic keyboard.*

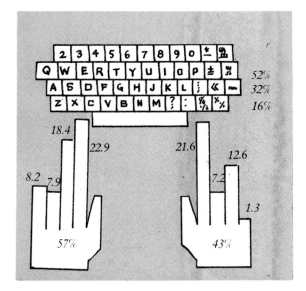

different design is the Maltron keyboard. But there are so many people who know how to use 'QWERTY' that the new keyboards are not usually wanted.

But as computers get smaller, ergonomists are turning their minds to designing a small keyboard which can be operated fluently and accurately with only one hand on a small pad.

Instead of having keys like a conventional typewriter, some keyboards are completely flat, with the characters printed on a washable plastic sheet, while some others have 'domes' made from metal or silicone rubber, which collapse when they are pressed. Many calculators and pocket computers have rubber dome switches. The domes usually have a plastic button on top.

Top *A flat, touch-sensitive keyboard.*
Above *Layout of a traditional QWERTY keyboard (left) and an alternative (Dvorak) keyboard. The percentages show the frequency of use of hands and digits.*
Below *A single-handed keypad.*

Visual displays

The commonest way – and a convenient one – for computers to display information is on a video screen.

Microcomputer

The cathode ray tube (CRT) in a TV set or video display unit (VDU) displays information by projecting a beam at a screen coated with phosphor. The beam scans across the screen from side to side and top to bottom, fifty to sixty times a second, causing the phosphor to glow until the beam reaches it again – otherwise the screen would flicker. A microprocessor controls the beam so that the screen displays characters in the form of glowing dots of phosphor.

A home computer often uses a TV set for its visual display. But because the computer's signal has to be converted into the signals on which television is broadcast, the display loses clarity and is comparatively fuzzy. So home computers often give only forty characters or less in a line, fewer than you would use if you were typing. This enables the characters to be larger than usual and therefore more legible.

If the computer's signal is connected more directly to the display, the clarity is better. Such a display is called a monitor. Often a monitor is integrated with a keyboard,

Above *A home computer often uses a TV set for its visual display.*
Below *A desk-top microcomputer for business use.*

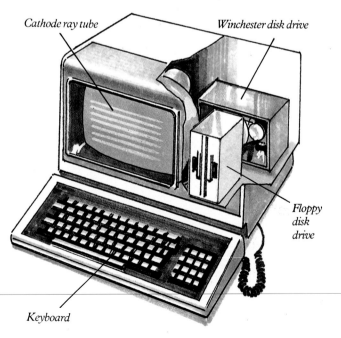

Cathode ray tube　　　　　*Winchester disk drive*

Floppy disk drive

Keyboard

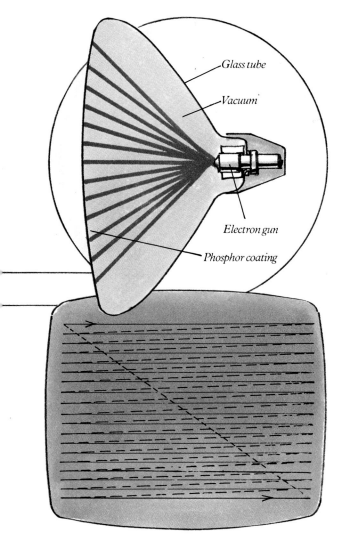

Glass tube

Vacuum

Electron gun

Phosphor coating

and then it is called a VDU. In a lot of microcomputers, the microprocessor and even the disk drives are put in the same box as the VDU – the video screen takes up so much room that the other parts can fit around it quite easily.

Some screens display information like the pages in a book, with black characters on a white background. You can even move 'pages' around the screen, put one in front of another, and magnify them or make them smaller.

Screens can also be in colour, but most work microcomputers, as opposed to home ones, use only one colour for the characters – white, green, orange or brown – against a grey background.

Because CRTs are big and heavy, scientists are trying to develop smaller ways of displaying information. The Sinclair flat screen, for example, projects the beam from the side, rather than from the back, then reflects it on to the phosphor on the back of the screen. So the whole screen can be quite thin or flat, because it does not have the glass tube projecting out the back.

Top *Cross-section through a cathode ray tube (CRT).*
Middle *How the cathode ray scans the screen.*
Below left *Close-up of the characters displayed on a CRT.*
Below *The Sinclair flat screen.*

Flat displays

The work of a room full of computers twenty years ago can be accomplished by a computer the size of a paperback book today. However, a screen based on a CRT has not reduced in size so dramatically, and takes up a lot more space than a paperback-sized book.

Below *Although a computer can now be as small as a paperback book, one page of the paperback will display more information than the computer's video screen.*

How can computer displays be shrunk down to the same size as a small computer? Liquid crystal displays (LCDs) may be the answer. Some special crystals, which are normally a transparent liquid, change to a dark colour when an electric current is passed through them behind special, polarized glass. Lines and dots of liquid crystal can be encased in plastic, wired up to a microprocessor, and used to display information. The wiring and control circuitry is complicated, so LCDs, at the moment, tend to be limited to small areas, such as watches and a couple of lines of display on portable computers.

Liquid crystals also have the advantage of using very little power – that is why a

Below *A liquid crystal display (LCD).*

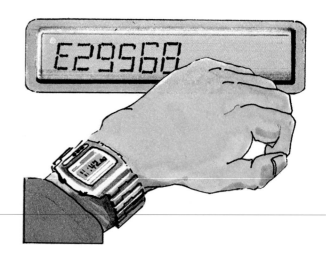

digital watch can run for years, displaying information all the time, on a very small battery. Over the next few years, scientists will be working hard to refine LCDs so that they can produce smaller liquid crystal dots on larger screens.

Light emitting diodes (LEDs) are like very small light bulbs, so you can see them in the dark, which you cannot with LCDs. They used to be used in watches, but are now mainly used in indicator lights, in calculators, and in electronic computer games. They use a lot more power than LCDs and so they need bigger batteries or power supplies.

Gas plasma displays, or fluorescent gas discharge displays, are also starting to be used. Dots of fluorescent gas light up when electricity is passed through them. But although their displays are very clear, they are bulky because of the control circuitry and the high voltage electricity they need. This means they need large batteries or power supplies. Electroluminescent displays work in a similar way, but need less electricity.

Usually, displays present information to the eye, but they can also present information for the touch sensation. Blind people use the Braille alphabet, which depicts the different letters of the alphabet by patterns of raised dots. A Braille display presents information in the same way by using a system of pins which the fingers can 'read'.

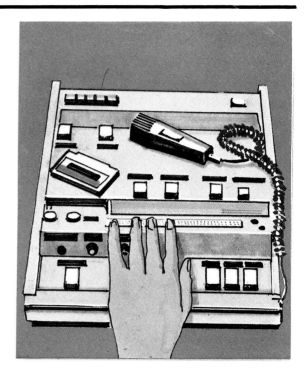

Above *How a Braille reader is used.*

Below left *A light emitting diode (LED) display.*
Below *A gas plasma display.*

Printing things

Output is often printed on paper, and it is then called hard copy. It has advantages over a VDU: you can fold it up and put it in your pocket, scribble notes on it, and read it without the aid of a machine.

The cheapest type of printer is a matrix printer. Matrix is a word often used in computers. It means something with rows and columns – like a football pools coupon, a calendar, or a railway timetable. A matrix printer has a battery of needles one above the other. Each needle produces a dot on the paper as the print head moves across the paper. In an impact matrix printer, the

Right *A small dot matrix printer for use with personal computers.*
Below *A daisy-wheel printer for use with business computers.*

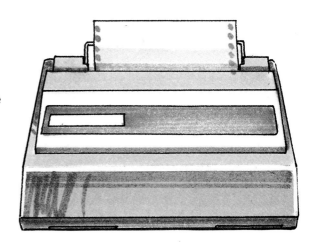

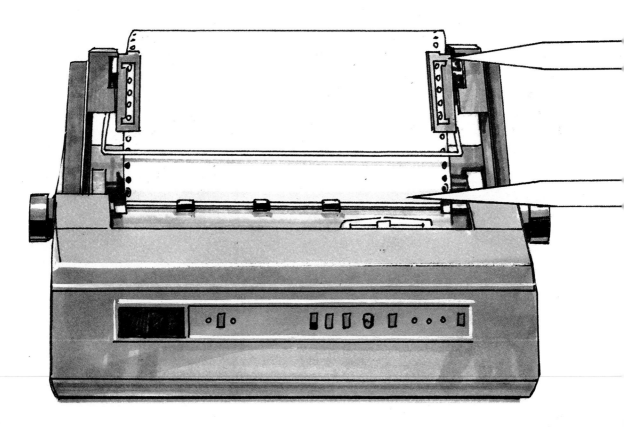

needles are moved sharply to mark the paper through a typewriter-style ribbon.

A thermal printer passes an electric current through the print head to make a mark on heat-sensitive paper. Thermal printers are often quicker, quieter and cheaper to buy than impact matrix printers, but they need special, more expensive paper.

Another type of impact printer is the letter-quality printer, which generally uses a daisy-wheel. This produces print which looks like typewriter print. Some daisy-wheel printers can do proportional spacing – they change the amount of space for each letter so that an 'i', for example, takes up less space than an 'm'.

Daisy-wheels can be changed to accommodate different styles of type. Daisy-wheel printers are usually much more expensive than matrix printers, and slower and noisier.

Matrix printers can also often print graphics – patterns, graphs and charts, or even complete pictures made up of individual dots. Some daisy-wheel printers can do this, too, but it is very laborious to build up an image by printing hundreds of single full-stops.

Printers can print at speeds from about thirty characters per second (about twenty-five lines per minute) upwards. A matrix printer might produce 100 characters per second, over a page in a minute. A bi-directional printer prints one line forwards and the next line backwards, so saving the time which the print head would take to go back to the beginning of the line.

Top left *Close-up of the characters generated by the dot matrix printer.*
Middle left *This tractor feed mechanism is used to pull continuous lengths of paper through the daisy-wheel printer.*
Left *A daisy-wheel print element.*

More input and output

Keyboards, screens and printers are the usual ways of putting information into computers and getting it out. But there are a wide variety of other ways, too.

Left *Digital weighing machines are fast replacing traditional (analog) scales.*
Below *A digital micrometer for very accurate measurements.*

A computer controlling a central heating system or a machine needs to get information from various sensors. But this brings a problem.

Computers work digitally, that is, they count in steps, each of which must be recorded as bits, the 0's and 1's of the computer. But the real world usually moves gradually, rather than in steps.

For instance, air temperature rises and falls in a continuous change, and the mercury in a thermometer also moves smoothly up and down. This gradual type of change is called analog. An analog watch is one with hands which move smoothly; a digital watch has figures which change one by one. An

analog weighing machine has a needle which moves to show the correct weight. A digital one has a display which shows the weight in, say, 1 gram steps. There are even some rare computers which work with analog signals.

Generally, computers work digitally so they have to be able to convert gradual

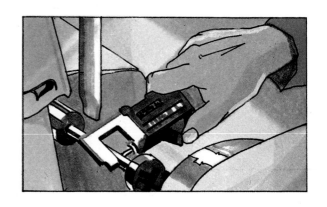

movement into digital information which they can deal with. The computer usually does this by using an analog-digital converter to interpret the signal that it gets from a sensor.

So a computer which is measuring temperature, weight, pressure or length will usually be converting an analog signal into a digital one.

Analog signals are used for control as well as for measurement. A joystick, for example, which is sometimes used for games or for moving a cursor – a flashing light – around a screen, uses analog signals. So does a mouse (a small mouse-shaped object on wheels), which can be rolled about on a computer desk to cause the cursor to move about on the computer's screen. This can be quicker and more accurate than moving the cursor by using the keyboard.

Video screens can also be used for input. You can touch a light pen, which has a photoelectric cell in the end, to a particular area of a screen. The pen registers when the beam in the CRT scans past it, and so can tell exactly where on the screen the beam is printing. A similar pen is used to read bar codes – the lines which you find on groceries to identify them for computers.

Screens can also have arrays of photoelectric emitters and receivers at the top and bottom and at the sides of them. When you touch the screen with your finger, you break one of the beams from top to bottom and one from side to side, so that the computer can work out where you are touching.

The computer input and output devices which have been covered so far have dealt

Top left *A joystick for playing electronic games.*
Left *A light pen in use on a video screen.*

33

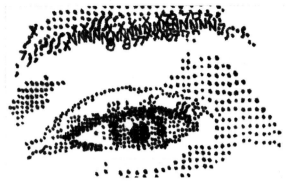

with text – with letters, characters and numbers. But computers can also handle complicated pictures and diagrams.

Pictures and lines can be 'digitized', that is, turned into the 0 and 1 signals that the computer can deal with. You may have seen the 'computerized pictures' that are sometimes done commercially. A video camera scans the scene – your face perhaps – and digitizes it. It does this by dividing up the scene into small blocks and looking in turn at each one, measuring how bright the area is. An analog/digital converter converts the measurement into the 0's and 1's which the computer can process and store. In fact, there is even a camera which works in this way instead of taking a picture on to a film as usual.

There are also pads or tablets which convert lines into digital signals. You write on the pad which is actually two sheets of plastic separated by a thin space. In one version the sheets are printed with thin wire lines, one sheet going vertically, the other going horizontally. When a pencil, pen or stylus presses on it the wires touch. The computer counts which horizontal line and which vertical line touch, and so can tell exactly where the pen is as it moves across the pad.

Other pads use a signal from a pen on a wire, similar to a light pen, to tell whereabouts the pen is. With any of these pads you can draw pictures and a computer will store them so that it can print them on its screen or alter them using a program.

Some of these pads can even recognize handwriting. They follow the movements of your pen over the tablet and then compare that movement with the pattern of particular letters. If the pattern matches, the computer recognizes the letter which has been written.

Left *Close-up of a photographic image (middle), and the same close-up as generated by a computer printer (top).*

Above *A pad which can read handwriting in use at a bank cash point.*
Right *Computerized design and typesetting. The words are entered through a keyboard into the typesetting machine, and the positions of the pictures are plotted on a pad.*
Below *Graph plotters can produce a variety of diagrams.*

Plotters are used for printing out lines, graphs, drawings and diagrams. Sometimes they print electrostatically, using the same principle as a photocopier. Other machines draw with a pen on an arm. Sometimes the plotter can even pick up and put down different coloured pens automatically! Each tiny electrostatic dot, or tiny movement of the plotter's arm is controlled by a single bit of information.

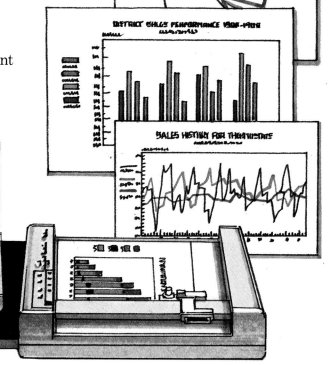

Computers talking together

One of the most important uses for computers is to send data from one to another. It is important because computers can send information very quickly and cheaply and over both long and short distances.

Microcomputers generally deal with eight or sixteen bits of information in parallel, that is to say, along eight or sixteen wires or paths at the same time, synchronizing their movement by the beat of a computer clock.

But data can also move serially all along the same wire, one bit following the other. The part of the computer that is sending the information, and the part of the computer that is receiving it, must agree both on how fast the data is coming, and on how many bits there are in each item of data. Serial transmission, as this is called, has the advantage that it needs only one piece of wire in order to carry the data, instead of eight or sixteen. But it is much slower than parallel transmission, although it may still be fast enough for most purposes.

Computer data can also be sent in the form of infrared rays over short distances. This is like the remote control on some televisions. Pulses of infrared light are sent out from an LED, and a detector senses the pulses. Ultrasonic waves (sound waves too high-pitched for humans to hear) can be used in the same way.

Radio waves are also used, so that computer data can be bounced off satellites across the oceans, just like television signals. Fibre optic cables, which channel laser light down thin, glass-fibre tubes, can carry large numbers of different signals.

Computers can also 'talk' down telephone lines. To do this they have to use

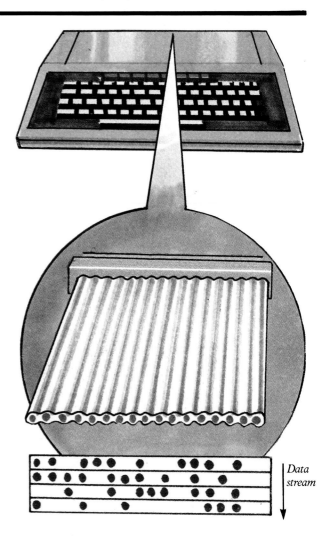

Data stream

Above *Microcomputers generally deal with data that is transmitted in parallel.*

a device called a modem, which changes the electronic pulses so that they can be heard and so transmitted over the phone. A modem can either be plugged into the telephone line itself, or connected via an acoustic coupler, which has cups which fit over the telephone handset.

Computers can even dial each other and answer the phone automatically. So a computer burglar alarm can phone the police without a human doing the dialling. And two computers can be programmed to send each other data in the middle of the night, when telephone calls are cheaper.

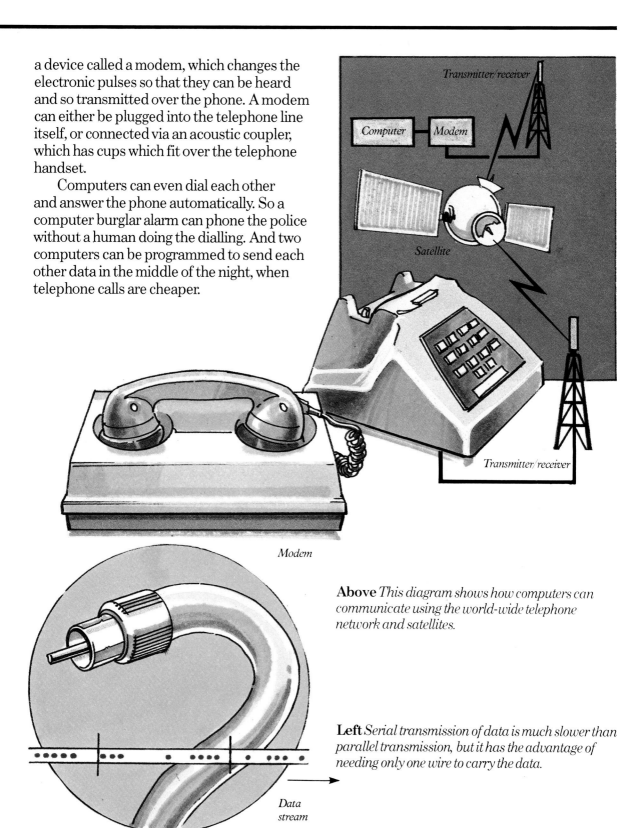

Transmitter/receiver

Computer *Modem*

Satellite

Transmitter/receiver

Modem

Above *This diagram shows how computers can communicate using the world-wide telephone network and satellites.*

Left *Serial transmission of data is much slower than parallel transmission, but it has the advantage of needing only one wire to carry the data.*

Data stream

Talking with computers

In future we will often talk to computers and computers will talk back to us. Instead of typing instructions and data into a computer we will dictate them out loud. The technology to do this already exists.

Before a computer can understand your voice it has to turn it into digital data. This process is called voice recognition.

Special chips can turn the analog signals of your voice into ditigal patterns via a microphone. When you talk you make a variety of sounds, and not just a single note. The chips turn these sounds into digital patterns, which it can then store as data.

For a computer to speak, it carries out the opposite process. Voice synthesis, as it is called, enables a computer to put together voice sounds from the digital codes which have been stored. Although not all the sounds

Above *A man dictating instructions and data into a computer.*

are reproduced, the computer gives a complete enough variety of sounds, so that it is hard to tell the difference between the computer's voice and a human voice.

Although it is not difficult for a computer to digitize a voice sound, record it, and recreate it in computer speech, it is much more difficult for it to understand what it has been told. It has to break the digital data up into patterns, and compare them with patterns that it already holds in its memory.

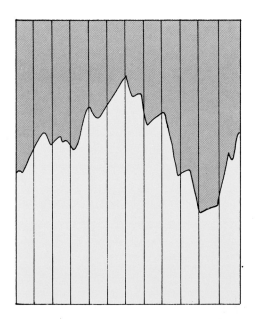

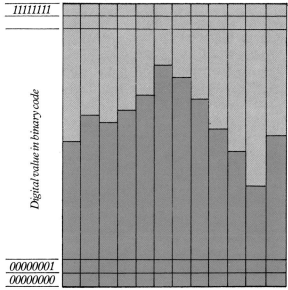

Digital value in binary code

11111111

00000001
00000000

they may have to be trained to recognize the voice of a particular operator. The operator will have to practice each sound several times so that the computer can store the patterns.

In future, computers will have telephones built into them. You will then be able to use the computer to dial numbers and to give messages. Computers will even carry on conversations, giving and collecting information and responding to the person on the other end of the telephone line.

Voice recognition will improve, so that training will not be needed. But we will not be able to do away completely with keyboards. It may not be possible to talk into computers, for example, when there is a lot of background noise. But keyboards will be used less than they are today.

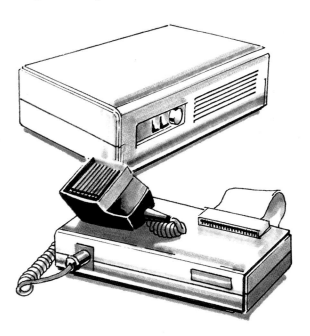

In normal speech many words are run into each other. This makes it difficult for the computer to tell what is the beginning of one word and what is the end of another. The computer also has difficulty working out the context of what you are saying. Even if it can recognize the sound 'red' it can't necessarily tell whether you mean 'red' or 'read'.

Computers also find it difficult to recognize a particular word spoken by different voices and in different accents. So

Top left *A simplified diagram of the waveform produced by the human voice.*
Middle left *The same waveform converted to digital form.*
Above *Voice input and output devices.*

Bigger machines

The computers that we have talked about so far have been micro-computers – a number of integrated circuits packed into a box small enough to fit on a desk. But until recently the word 'computer' meant something much bigger.

A few years ago a computer was a whole room full of boxes, and there are still big computers like this today, called mainframes. These have several times the memory that microcomputers have, and work several hundred times faster.

Big computers used to work as batch machines. This meant that all the data and programs were fed in at the start of a 'run' and all the results came out together at the end. You could not see anything happening whilst it was running, and if you had made any

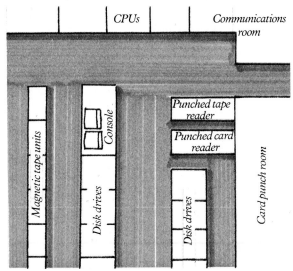

Above *A typical mainframe installation.*
Right *Layout of a mainframe installation.*

mistakes in programming or entering the data, you would only find out later.

Then minicomputers came along. These were smaller – but still usually needed an air-conditioned room to themselves – and allowed timesharing. The work of the CPU was shared between a number of people – all working at the same time but on different terminals. The computer cleverly attended to each person in turn, and did this so fast that each user could think that the computer was not working for anybody else.

Minicomputers are still used, although microcomputers are now so cheap that it really is possible to have your computer devoted to you and to you alone. With minicomputers you can have a lot more memory and disk storage, and you can share expensive peripherals like very fast printers.

It is also true that some people are only using minis and mainframes because they started doing so before micros were available.

In any case, by linking micros together in networks you can still share expensive peripherals.

Minis and mainframes often use bits of equipment which you rarely see on a micro. Punched card machines, for instance, date from the days before time sharing and before VDUs became common. Instead of keying programs and data into a VDU, card punch

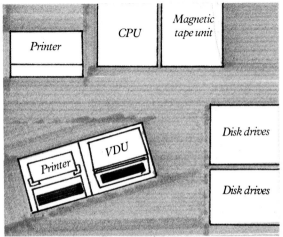

Above *A typical minicomputer system.*
Left *Layout of a minicomputer system.*

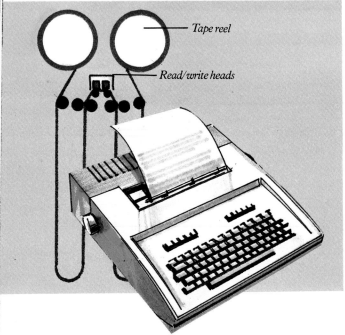

Tape reel

Read/write heads

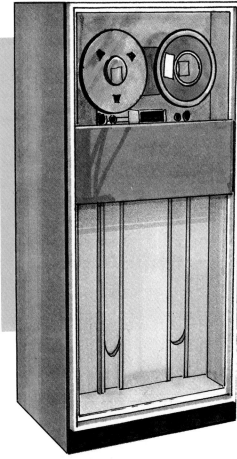

Above *A magnetic tape unit (left), and a diagram showing how the tape reels and read/write heads are arranged. The loops of tape allow the tape reels to stop and start very quickly.*
Above right *A teletype machine.*

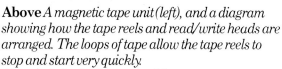

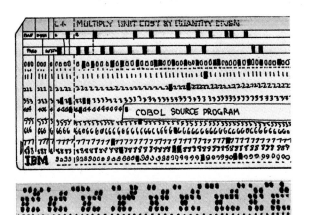

operators use a keyboard at a machine which punches holes in cards. Each hole position represents one bit of information.

Then all the cards are stacked together and put into a card reader, so that the computer can read in their information. It does this by pushing the cards past photoelectric cells whilst light is being shone on them. When a cell can see light through a hole in the card, the card reader registers its position and translates that as information for the computer. A stack of cards would be a batch of programs or data. It is easy to make a mistake with punched cards and they can be lost and damaged, so they are used less and less.

Punched paper tape is also used in the same way, except that it is a continuous stream of tape instead of separate cards. But magnetic tape and disks are much easier to use.

Left *Data prepared for input to the computer on a punched card (top) and paper tape.*

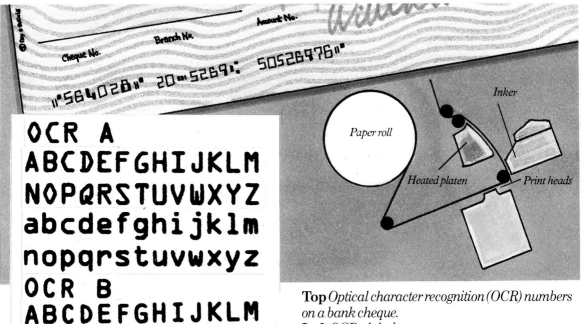

Top *Optical character recognition (OCR) numbers on a bank cheque.*
Left *OCR alphabets.*
Above *Main components of a printer based on the Xerox copying process.*

Before VDUs became the normal way of putting information into a computer, machines like typewriters, called Teletypes, were used. These are very slow and noisy compared with a modern matrix printer, and much less convenient to type on than typing with a screen. But many of them are still being used.

Big computers, like the smallest home computers, often use magnetic tape to store information. This tape is on large reels and is read from and recorded on very much faster than a little tape cassette.

Occasionally, computers have machines which enable them to read the printed word. Optical character recognition (OCR), as this is called, sometimes has to use specially shaped characters, like those on bank cheques. These are easier for the computer to recognize. But there are now cleverer machines which can read ordinary print and typed reports. They scan the page with a laser beam, digitize it, and compare the patterns that they find with other patterns that they

have been programmed with. If the pattern they look at matches the pattern stored for the letter 'A', then they know that it must be an 'A'.

Big computers also use other more expensive types of printers, which can often print very fast indeed, as much as 40,000 lines a minute! That is nearly 1,000 pages a minute! Ink-jet printers squirt microscopic droplets at the paper and deflect them electrostatically to shape characters.

Other printers are based on the Xerox copying process, or on lasers. An older technique is to have rapidly revolving chains or bands of characters, where the characters are hit by hammers when they are opposite the right place on the paper.

All these printers are too expensive to use with micros at the moment. But remember that the mainframes of twenty years ago were less powerful than your microcomputer today – and in a few years' time you will probably be able to get a micro as powerful as today's big mainframes.

Glossary

Aerodynamic Shaped to pass easily through air.

American Standard Code for Information Interchange (ASKII) A Computer code for representing characters.

Analog Refers to a gradual type of change rather than change in the form of steps which can be counted. The opposite to digital.

Arithmetic and logic unit (ALU) Part of the central processing unit of a computer, where calculations and logical operations are done.

Array A group of symbols or numbers arranged in rows or columns, or as a single column or a row.

Binary Counting to base two.

Bit The smallest unit of information, a 0 or a 1 in the computer.

Byte A byte is made up of eight bits. A megabyte is one million bytes.

Capacitor An electronic component which holds electricity for a period.

Cathode ray tube (CRT) A glass tube which displays information by projecting a beam at a screen.

Central processing unit (CPU) The unit of a computer in which processing of data takes place.

Circuit A collection of electric or electronic components having wires or links between them. An integrated circuit has all these components and links on one silicon chip.

Computer A machine which gets information, changes and organizes it, stores it, and puts it out in a new form when needed.

Data The information which a computer deals with.

Decimal Counting to base ten.

Dedicated Used for specific purposes.

Digital Working in digits or numbers. The opposite to analog.

Electroluminescent display A display which uses a relatively small amount of electricity to activate a light-emitting gas.

Electronic Having to do with electricity, but using components like transistors and vacuum tubes (valves) to control the current.

Electrostatic Having a static electric charge – the charge obtained by rubbing a balloon or a plastic comb, for example.

Emitter Something which puts out or emits electricity.

Etch To eat away a surface with a chemical, usually to a specific design.

Gas plasma display A display using a gas which glows when electricity is passed through it.

Gate A circuit, made up of transistors, which controls the flow of data in a computer.

Infrared The part of red light which is invisible to the naked eye, but can be picked up by sensitive instruments.

Input The information which is put into a computer.

Integrated circuit *See* **Circuit**

Joystick A stick which is sometimes used for moving a cursor – a flashing light – around a computer screen. Joysticks are often used with computer games.

Logic A system of reasoning where a particular set of inputs will predictably produce a particular set of outputs.

Megabyte *See* **Byte**

Microcomputer A computer based on a microprocessor. While a microcomputer usually means a complete microcomputer system with input, output and storage, the word is sometimes used for the actual microprocessor chip.

Microprocessor A term which is normally used to mean the single chip containing the central processing unit, but it can also be used to mean the complete microcomputer system.

Output The results which come out of a computer after processing.

Oxide A material which has been changed through oxidization.

Oxidize To change the surface of a material by putting it in contact with oxygen.

Peripheral A computer device which is separate from the computer itself.

Photoelectric Electronic signals converted from light waves.

Photoelectric cell A device which converts light waves into electronic signals.

Printed circuit board (PCB) An insulating board which has circuits printed on it. Electronic components are connected by these circuits.

Probe A pointed object used to touch things which are difficult to get at.

Processor The part of the computer where the processing is done. If the processor is on a single chip it will be called a microprocessor.

Program Instructions which are written into a computer to make it work.

Resistor A component which resists the passage of electricity.

Sensor A device for sensing something that is happening – for reading fluctuating temperatures or light levels, for example.

Serial Moving after each other, one by one.

Solder A mixture of tin and lead which, when heated to melting point, can be used to join some metals.

Stylus A pointed object used for writing or drawing, but without ink.

Synthesis The process of putting together objects or ideas.

Terminal A device separate from a computer for keying in information and displaying it.

Transformer A device for transforming electricity from one voltage to another.

Transistor An electronic component which can be used as a switch.

Video display unit (VDU) A terminal where data is displayed on a screen rather like a television screen.

Volt The unit used to measure the force of electricity.

Finding out more

Books

You may want to start finding out more about computers by reading the other books in this series:

Computers in Everyday Life tells how computers will be used around the home and in everyday life.

The Story of Computers tells of their history and development.

Computers and You talks about how they are affecting the society in which we live, our way of life, and the problems and benefits they bring.

Programming Computers talks about the languages we use to get computers to work for us.

Robots and Intelligent Machines is about computers at work and on the move.

If you browse in your local book store or library you will find a number of other books on computers. Titles to look for on how computers work include *Illustrating Computers* by Colin Day and Donald Alcock (Pan Information, 1982); *Fred Learns about Computers* (Macdonald Evans, 1981); and *Microfuture* by John Shelley (Pitman, 1981).

Books about computers in general include *Scelbi's Secret Guide to Computers* by Russell Walter (Scelbi, 1981); *The Computer Book* from the BBC, (BBC,1981); and *The Personal Computer Book* by Robin Bradbeer (Gower Publishing Company, 1982).

Magazines

There are a number of general magazines about microcomputers, in which people sometimes write about the way computers are affecting our lives. British magazines include *Personal Computer World* and *Practical Computing. Computing Today* specializes in the computer hobbyist. *Microcomputer Printout* is also good. American magazines include *Byte, Interface Age* and *Microcomputing.*

A number of magazines concentrate on home computers, including *Your Computer,* and *Computer and Video Games,* in the UK.

For people who have got a particular microcomputer, there are also many magazines which deal with individual popular models.

Computers

You can also use computers to find out about computers. In the UK *Prestel* carries computer programs and information about clubs (which you can also get from some of the computer magazines).

Computerized Bulletin Boards are also spreading in several countries. Your computer talks to another computer over the telephone, and you can look at messages and fetch games and programs on to your own computer. You may be able to do this from your school, although somebody will have to pay for the telephone call!

Index

Index